Micrographia

Micrographia

Emily Wilson

University of Iowa Press

Iowa City

University of Iowa Press, Iowa City 52242

Copyright © 2009 by Emily Wilson

www.uiowapress.org

Printed in the United States of America

Design by Sara T. Sauers

The University of Iowa Press is a member of Green Press
Initiative and is committed to preserving natural resources.

Printed on acid-free paper

LCCN: 2008935531

ISBN-13: 978-1-58729-801-1

ISBN-10: 1-58729-801-5

09 10 11 12 13 P 5 4 3 2 1

for Mark

Contents

« iii »

« i »

Fugitive

Take down what is left
of the leaves.

Shred them off with a workmanship
there so it is done.

Rose-yellowed underneath what is now
more rose than rubiate.

Tinged at the tips
the personage of the field

coming clear by the foment
moving through it.

Look up through the radial describe.
A cloud is decaying.

It disbands from itself.
It is the law.

Morpho Terrestre

The butterfly is pinned through its thorax
and from that point the wings read
in canted panels
releasing the stored chromes
the inner mechanics.
The name affixes to earth.
The wings barely do.
Watchet blues of the tingeing substance
trapped in the plates of Muscovy-glass
nudged free in time with elegant twists of the nib.
The design of the wing permits
its partial retraction—
vague shallowing folds—
wing worked up from a packet of dampened acetates—
so there can be semblance
to begin with at night against the bark of a tree.
Brush of the foot to the mottled bark,
filling-in patches of drab
on the celadon vine, the minimum
pattern permitting.
The legs have been plucked,
feelers sealed back from the jaws with dark glue.
Makeshift road of the sleeper
plied through the gorge.

Interior

reflections in a marriage breakfront
in which to glimpse a door

has just been opened
a child come half-way through

then backed back in again
or outside arms of red cedars

I must think before thinking of them
so limber road-red and persisting

around to some mean
I must go toward through snow

barrens above an ocean
the cognitions of which give of

shales of greens of
things I know dwell there

Small Study

Sparrows swiveling the feeder
so the seed whorls
so the dove can come from its fix
in the waver of cedars.
Some one makes a husk note
that a pair can flare into as if
built from that scutch
of the undergrowth—
roughening birds, birds skimming into
slits they fit into in trees between
loads of the branches—
through paths
through encampment
go dozens who work the steep yews
combing the motes of the dove or
milling its ground, shifting its bandings
of gray and mole gray, taupe and slate gray
beginning to scuff
into lozenges, drab and saxe blue—
one of them nicking
the field where there's tilt
off center
flocked in the shreds of new balsam
or come from the rendering
junctions or sorts through the deal—
afterward seamed in the fledge—
coal and flush gray, fuse and rush wove or
let go

Endemic

Smoke layering off the warehouse
and behind it the highway's
swift river.
Recession again through Bill's garden
always the mid-ground
complex rigged wildness.
The fence grizzled with lichen.
It rickets around the whole place
it flexes where the bulk of the branches
moves up against it.
Hard little bittersweet foils
spiraling the ruminant lilac bush.
Rain coming in and then pigeons
and squirrels squalling off along the fence top.
And Bill coming in once
to pin a shirt to the strung-across line
once to take stock of the actual
patch he puts lettuce in, turnips, tomatoes
the casual, centripetal banner beans.
All that's beginning to show
through the gray cages of the lilacs
through back-tracking colleges
of brambles, forsythia and witchgrass.
Between it among it forced under it
shocked and multiplying
certain the estrangement.

Camperdown Elm

the little-boned
complex underthing
that is private
stemming toward a leaf

breaks open in
such flukes such ochers
such
within its armature
are you here
are you not with me

somewhere in that
enjambment within
a cave within the brain
small-glittering
incremented

about to spread outside
itself construed
in a sense there too
a tree

Monadnock

Sometimes the whole thing stands
still, residual
ribbed as the stratum is
of the branchwork.
You are given the gruff versus
the seams and you must drop back
to recapture its stranded
cloudcap.
Fire, fire and fire, all toothed
in the obelisk spruces.
It seems to be listing,
burled in the surface.
The purple adheres to the back
pivots, shunts over
the scotched hump.

No. It thrusts up burgeoning
finer-tined, the parts more mobile-like.

So the eye has no end
going on outside its compulsion.
Then the colors coruscate also.
Then what does the bulk of it do.
A rudiment-hoard.
Then what.

Motif

There's still a little sun
we can cross over

you will have to stand
the etched bloom on

the capture pond
I will have to stand for

the emplacement
russet in its creases

the referential cedar which
approaches like

the wood
of wild turkeys in that

ruche of leaves they leave in
shooting off

Little Gothic

We rode on a road through a wood
The wood itself rode along a river
Slow beige wade of mid-passage
Between regions of our union
In the form of a forest of tulip trees

We rode on a road of seepages
Bridged with viridians
Sun took pause, low down
What was almost gold

We rode crossed with roads
Closing in and paths that were more
Like pressures
Wild harts. Soldiers.
A far little stage stung with figures
A box with a breakdown at the bottom

Just that the road moved off sequence
The forest bore out its own office
Its own kind of craft
We rode through the wood along the river
Beyond the mineral
Over-richness that leads off
An inwardness

Event

Snow in the coils
of the vine in the traceries

of the lilac breaks down in
loose chunks that are pitting

the snow they fall into
whose rule is now lateral

pendence of crystals now hitched now
struck under

inside is the African violet
strain of the underleaf

almost magenta recessed
toward the stalk I think

what the substance
urged into

Sunset: Rouen?

Just to the left and down from
the central engagements
—clock-tower, vaults of the long mauve bridge
sun and its correlate
swashes come back
to prime, spurred
cathedral, ceding
carmine, chartreuse up against it.
The horses stand in their traces.
Their wagon floats at the dark wharf-fringe.
Fused through the loads,
watermarks, persons or poles,
soldered spots that are shadows
or breaks at the junctures of reeds,
scarcely at home in themselves, stationing there,
forced to make reddish banks red
they have been horses—
the fixing of them in grit-grass—
strangely set off.
Ramparts ruck over the underside slips.
What are they waiting for?
The edge of the picture unsettles,
tricks itself forth
like the passage in which is restored
your miniature boy
ritually combed and folded.
A few fawn strokes still to be
harbored as horses.

Growth and Form

The bittersweet tethers the lilac
training away the festoons

away from the sun, sun in its hamper of clouds
something comes under the protean

rights, weird rights of the fine tent skeleton
which now has the mind full of

torque enforcing the burgundy closures of the cones
the bittersweet blots out

all the rubrics the rain touches into
Bill's garden, raw garden

Stereotype

There is Homer's studio
white-mullioned, just above the scrawl
scrub-rose, sumac and juniper clambered over
red-yellow sticklers you pick
suddenly up among the branches
in denser encroaches of branches
down to the rocks.
It is possible to make out
the stops in the cockling stone
almost monochrome
wedgwood, jouvence blue, blue woad
where the wave funds up
expressed from an undergone
trough, the pedestals
sloughing off echoes, "crumbs" and "tumblers."
It insists on its own kind of fixture
originally I mean
the tourmaline sheets giving way
in shocked foam
broken down in the vats of
black rocks so you lose all sense
of even just the momentary
executions—
remote cylinders, cone
stunts of the headlands

Prospect

It grew at that slant
alone, down there
beneath the cordons
of pitch pines
some lapse in definition
unsteadying
the trunk state—
the bristled shot branch
deposits its blossoms through branches.
The parts have no portion why not?
They cannot be counted why not?
They make the thing whole?
It grew at that slant.
Tints flashing up
from the buds
from the scaling off
barks, sap in the germ-slots of cones.
It had to stoop to come up.
A thing can't be saved from its parts?
It had to be blunt.
It grew at that slant.
And blooms back up in the branches.

« ii »

Blue Hill

Built of the silicate actions of a grass

of a shade of the locketing groves that are shattering

in the thoughts of the lavender pageant so we fell

gutted in a field in an artifact of the hand that sows outward

out-spreading for the spire of a cypress

particular so help me in its stead

Poem

The moment of the loam in its plot.
Of the slatted fence.
Of the jay's flanged ceruleans bearing through branches.
The moment of my grid and of my pick.
The tamarind trim, the smart old man's trim.
The moment persisting in the picture.
Encroaching on its rule.
The yard set around with windows
in-fitted with buildings, with happenings.
Edgework, extractions, off-structures,
intrusions of the thicketing lilacs and bittersweet
vines that fix over them and staggers
of blackberry cane that Bill has let go there.
All the plexure my neighbor Bill has let go there.
The moment of a relative openness.
Then the sheared moment along the roof line.
Then taking the near passage toward the street.
The thought of taking a swift walk up the street
toward the outlook above the highway
from which won't I see the ice has stacked up
against the cove banks like custard glass again like the
softened whole regions
that are broken and fused and refused with the sea's
slow momentums.

Picturesque

Most acts, if they are acts
are not primary acts
amid the -taxis
of other actions
are they. Something
straying still beside the canal, bird
or birdlike rodent in its grip
before bidding—dart
and a bur-
bush sleeves it.
Scum-drift surface the surface
derives from its depth
some slabbish man-shadows
contained, figured in, then refigured
in blocks
impoundments.
And little guts appear
in walls and asphalt
pink disturbing
bursts, vascular
shafts, rotational
basal aigrettes like chamois insoles.
And factions of trees, roof-lots and bridge-lots.
The pull, the tack, and the load
up of buildings on trees, trees through the brackets
of buildings like ramparts through groves
fur-feathered groves giving furthermost arches, parterres
to reach and recede with

Little Discourse

The needles of art are blunt
but those of nature—
hawthorns, quills, mosquito bits—
sharp as needles under the scope
we invented ourselves for seeing
for we are rude and stumble Hooke said
in our displacements.

What I slip
between the gills of the organic
beautifactions, lifting the parts
apart to touch for eminences
mildews or smuts.

There is a dense prickling of ice
on the inner linings of the lilac
aglint with the slight break of the bush
in the move of the barest snowfall.

Through the yard of lilacs
comes the cardinal pair
one streaming red, one the barest
tensing of red which is almost gray,
gray radiance.
They are butting and switching among branches
come into the picture like drifters
who make the gathering more strange.
They work their way inside
the twigwork.

Spring Intensive

Little cruxes of the lilacs.
The light now filtering
through fog ignites the new wicks
of forsythia.

The device innovates inside itself
through a garden through a fog
expending its shadings and breakages
in the reflexes of being
the yellow stabwork.

It is the draw of the windows
all around it the extent of the watching
all across it all inside it or all through it.

Triggerings enveloping the fence-edge.
Flourishes, stays.
Forsythia and lilac and stricture.
The manner in which it fills in.
Wickedness. Tint.

Tableau

Speech, the slate-blue grooves
of the adolescent pigeon, its pinfeathers
ranked, preened, bitten over
constantly by the parent—
not by the stand-by nurselike
ancillary bird who keeps watch
watching the rugged front
of shrubs and daylight.
It all happens on the air-conditioner
in the "chimney" between back "wings"
of the brownstones, fidgeting
in the cote of twigs and pewter-dark shit.
A tool being worked
not sharp enough
to bore its way to the mark.
At times it goes quiet, a little crying, mostly faithless,
a little quiet.
It goes on around
the scalloped edge.
And there are slots down which can filter the cold, condensed.
And what of the claws?
And what of the fibrillate furl
resisting and generating
itself inside the snug jacket?
The text is four figures, inter-hitched
or something like that, brushed inside red rules
or what I do I do in my own office.
The nurse-bird, so familiar, do I know it
from the stage?, staying just
outside the nest, and the child-bird
stuffed beneath the mother or the mother
with the father battering upward, barely
catching tips but so they catch.

Coal Age

trunks budded and scarred
summer experience on the loess edge of the moraine

fallings out between elders
beautiful forestations of made language

put forth a little finger
on the tip in composite relief the damselfly structure exacted

a storm floats over the purchase
neither you nor I neither one of us

mass interlockings of leaves tiny waxed tabs interlapping
the false pines the puzzling pines

it has not yet occurred along the limb it has not yet
   determined to be spurlike
it is not yet done it lingers in the pattern of its advancement

are you long of this world I
am delivered into casting my bit among us

are you a being of more than one measure
ruffed so none can hold

Monoprint

snow that is slabbing
all the downdrift around it
settling and rounding
the outside worked in of
the macular golds
whoever has passed by the pole
passed through herself saying
is this the reel of the road
chiseled and sheared
a rumor flown from the coast
a network of creosote bushes
sprigging through sleep
took notice of this and moved on
tested the zone where this was
coming in slowly
went forth with the field unpinned
from the end
of a fretted ice tonsil
the bitter reward no one knew
died and went forth

Round the Mountain

rouge-wedged and bogs
built to the rims of

spillage stone that then gets stacked
in walls to keep in grazers, in

or out, the circuit cuts the sod, lobed
cushion plant flares out white

against its bronzing—
make a thing like that behave

it's okay to go alone
not okay it makes one selfish

snow melts
plumbing down the tiers

old man standing with us
take his picture so

he takes the jungle orange and
dry biscuit, round

the cuffs a
steady stirrup stitch

Zoetrope

False hellebore, lodged in the clefts
of the ravine we climbed up into
fanned shafts, looked down through shredded
cloud to the pit
of slid quartz.
Like a view I was given
of slots in a limestone wall
above Pisac, Peru
sconced with coppery fog-plants.
There are the vents of the buildings also
distinct among lofts
with their hawk settles
and their capstone logic.
The plains wrap out around them
capsules of ice
off the hot-metal front.
I would not go there.
High on the bluffs above the joint
of the brown and zinc rivers
in the silver-gel film down
which the monk must slip
in a little bark boat.

Johnny Rotten's Produce

At the backwater base
where staunch knotweed grows
Johnny Rotten sang a song
of sweet regard for he was rotten.
What produce there can be roves far from here
in typic mounds bristling
beyond the canal's steel groove.
Oily damascenes edge the greenish reflections—
of an island even?
One on which the structures float
among trucks and pallet stacks, plaster urns and flower pots.
Something off its stalks
exudes, drops
like the least terns dropping to dense water
wedged, boned in with the knotweed
that quirks the lock-water
along which junk trees flourish
drupe-like clusters
stobbed through the ribs of
green, green-orange, and green converges on the windows
of that train, aclimb
from the balking cement yard.
The thrill dwells dormantly down
the warped flutes of the canal, oh, absent abundance.
There is green to rent.
And to foreclose upon
and let tarnish in terraqueous canes.
The sign says Johnny Rotten.
And Preston's Tools withdraws
behind its scrim.

Watercolor with Scraping-Out

Those jots of fir
in passages of snow, snow-
endorsed gullies where the ridge drops
off, into what—
the hatch of light poles and
athletic-field fencing
that elm, its yellowish
ticking off from the strong-limbs.
There are people going over
all the time on occasion I imagine
trying to see where it chambers down
or out, the long ravine.
Where no roads go, paths go, and then
plaited ruts that end in a general
crescent—something broad
turned about, cracking the grass.
It resists?
It does not resist.
This time the clouds get their edges
vanished away from, banded in crops
corrugations.
They must be more certain
more ruled and scale into the iced cuts
of the parking lot.
Like a thought thought out
on its track
far off from myself
I may recall in plain sight—
sort of true, sort of tortuous—
cumulatively speaking
the darker grips
toward black.

Notchland

at the hinge of going over

firs vanish up washes
annealed

a mountain
on either side

out-drifts
loose in the arms

inelegant
meaning

loss of the complex
meaning

smeared in place
the place

tables up in windrows
clouds and under

rigs of cloud

« iii »

Micrographia

Not quite mosses
alike in their stints
frangible strands and branchings
crimps, crenulations
on a single stretch
you can pick out the patching
convolved
scrolling displays from the arched
twigs

it gets warmer
toward the bottom
of the basin
through the packets
of pines the whirring red pines
sulfurous spritz on the inside rim of the spring
implying slow growth

nuthatches counter with distal control
inserting their beaks in the bark
something blunt
suspected in surfeits of pitwork—
horsehair, gauzes, and tinsels streaked off
from the points
the further you go
the compounds absorb through the script
alike in divide and doubled-up
scope—rifle-crack fishbone-beard wind-shield
tungsten rosette, cursed
wolf lichen

The Yew

The neighbors' garden yew exceeds some closely
plotted things—hosta, roses, flagstones—
getting coarser in the base-line
drill of rain, "threads" of rain, "threads" of
exploration over an array
come of sprung needs
squirrels riding in on branches
to snag the bright arils
worked into vertiginous crooks
green-black axial slats
nature in this as it were expressing its thing
a plant grafted out of a pre-modern one
what can constrain it
the neighbors' dark dog
pits in the splinter-rich dirt, much closer than
it would appear
obscure, constructive
of what might appear
as bits in a rastered tableau
systems of dense entrainment
coming in close
hydrangea clouds broken in toxic patrols
of the yew
its slow-growing tight-grained alignments
so suited to javelins, ball-spikes and flexing red long bows
equipped with taxus-tipped darts
the "threads" the "threads" or
what could be run through the drone
of blotted-in blacks the black voided velvets
of hills where they burn
right down the furze cracks
or skewed in the flashing around the tarred
roof of the shed, shedwork of rain into
neighboring volumes

Pleasant Hill

The change is more a plateleting—
greens on silt-green, willows, alders

impactions of the field
beginning to catch

rain and snowmelt
inking out systems

leading to them
shorebirds, waterbirds

scratch inside the reeds
and on the higher drive

whose windows stack the sunset clouds
blurred raves, base ingots

concealed of all the works
coming down in stages

access-roads gone in
on both sides

Protea

The bracts drying and sharpening.
Bits of the bloom cured, revolute
tools to do the scoring.
Things turned in on themselves
surfaces that were hidden inside plumage
—jester, starlight, flame spike
gnarled shuttle-cock
the botched brokerage.
Linnaeus saw the sketched bud.
The recondite continents came.
Two cliffs, opposite-hinged, along which
sugarbirds browse for scarab beetles, seeds
snag inside the pins and are borne off.
The leather-lipped jack-fire feels
for stems underground—
garnets shrill in the schist, agardite
flock operates up gutters like dense moss.
Lumbering parts meet rarefied parts and suffer
each the other, otherwise
curled on the keels.
Half the time what was I thinking
undoing through the cup
around the rim.
The disparate wrought exposures,
extremely formed,
so I can't picture it myself
—at the foot of the bed
against the yellow wall
near the bowl of change and ticket stubs—
the grayish hoodish train of packed anthers,
mock-anthers?, wildly plush, rived
from the sheath.

Gray and Greens

I want to discern them
among them like you

multiplicate tones condensing
in dusk as sensate as one

can be the function of two
stroboscope rooms through

slipped definition or tincture or
blastwork of reeds

starched button spike the
burned-out track of a lotus

caught in the pads
a raw-grass-orpiment

bamboo slash at the bank
the heron come clean

back-hitched in the salve-
green willow

Synthetic Figment

All along it clustered thorns
derange at stark intervals
sleeked to the ends and
riding the wide trunk
like ships squat-sparred or like
the wreckages of ships.
Wild sweet locus.
Tree of agon.
I feel it divide
its nickel-toothed combs—
the night substance—
having something to do
with the obstinate whole
which needs must advance—
advance or force
back the background
racked up in squares
squared pairings and principal
stiffenings out from
the copped fuselage.
Or standing one part for the underrun
sylva rhetoricae through which the swamp
herds flow on hooves grown spatulate
for shallow digging.
It must be something else.
It must must be.
All along incorporating
the proud flesh.

Fidelity

to the native colors
to the knitting shadows that feed
the forward computations
artisanal
so there's downfallen
litter and gelatin
green in the olivine scruffs of the club moss.
The rock moves under its imprint
so I have to look away
to the rock with its warp
toward the base.
Fibrous escapes
through the rungs
of the up-dug roots.
Is it wrong to put forth
an encaustic pink along the gore-edge?
You'd have to live with it like that
in the gaps
that conclude
the spruce pool.
It's all very well and good
to put yourself forth.

The Spruce

It might actually be enmeshed.
It dazzles rather
withers the grass with dinted shade
densities figuring
what to see, blue, blue segments
the spruce
what is the bucked edge
come up against, girds, that is, unnatural
things I can't get into—
don't, don't mention it—
someone cries out in the theater
behind the wrecked swags
I go in
upon the spruce
by that repulsion—
singular forked shadows
where branches are
arrayed and meet the ground
in close duff rings
how far it goes
with its black knobs
getting into the street—
forcing slowly out to the bird-feeder's stake
the rough spruce-threads
working off from the form—
one awake to the other's
pushing through
smoke-cut, crystalled, sand-grit
the root hairs
crude and terminal
that make the spruce yield up

Spiral Bound

the way we would want them
streaked in the junks
as we would have them

the poles have been stripped tacked out one to one
at the five-fingered crossroads
none can be sure
which is

the rock is fibered like a meat—
gristle and plait
the wave nudged pink

both sides of the reach concede
timber-dark groups

now you can see the
exposed
second struts of

gray/violet

North

The river clips through the peat.
The peat holds the melt so well
it fills up the cuts.
Rills feed the loops' occasional
straight runs kept hard to a fault.
This is not "north."
The blur of the bank goes
brown, fust-brown.
Musk oxen pick out their route
through it, freshly described
where light is in play
in shreddings the water sends up.
The sea is in play.
What says it is north?
Plates of the mountains break down
in checkers and stains.
Their action is being
never quite there I'd know
what is there
around which the sun could resolve
a phalarope's egg
that holds its salt gob for the savor.
What marks the end of the notching in.
Snags of their wool
in the sheaf-rock.

Red-Legged Kittiwake

1

Native it seems to no part
of the North American continent
but some islets off
the rugged scarps of the Aleutians
in the loose entablatured cliffs
among dwarf-willow tips.
Known if at all by its silhouette
(we can know such things by their silhouettes)
the red-legged kittiwake
glimpsed in isolate parts of Oregon
California and southern Nevada
said to go silent in winter
slitting through snow
the red-legged kittiwake.

2

The red of the red-legged kittiwake
of a kinship with black
solders across the ice-gaps.
Native in no real part
but its obdurate course the red-
legged kittiwake goes silent.
We can know still more by rips
through the weed.
Red-legged kittiwake
gone back in the brain toward
noise of the narrowing ship-lanes.

3

Silver bones of the wrist
in their riggings rotate.
Pulp of the madder-root
shocked in white alum then soaked

through the wool for the waistcoat.
The frigate sprays back gray rime
cuts through the ice-skirt
pursuing such things
to the knit of the nest.

4

Crowberry swollen with fog
lichen resist on the lowest
spokes of the spruce
red-legged kittiwake
native to no part
alone in its parts

5

Kelp closes up
where the bird has just been

6

The legs retract in the pan
of the tail near the crotch
against the streaked ruff
bits of the barbs in breakage
out in the vanes
tipped into place
leaf of the willow tipped into
its branch the tip but tip to its whole

7

So where does it go when gone.
The wake of the factory ships.
Its chevrons compound the steep bluffs
it makes itself into those ranks
like pistons or books.
Its numbers are known to be in decline.
Is red for the advent
of sex or something more plain.

8

The sea works its surface.
Notched and convex.
It gives up its force in forms it must make.
It has a grease shine.
It is where they go when gone isn't it
through the known parts

Excursion

A plinth-land of pinkish rock
feldspars, we were told, fixed in
with paler, blacker stone, back in the middle eon.
We drove to see the ocean from that ground
more pendant-blue, with more striation
way out off the high old rocks
flushed and shimmed, at the ends of their erosion—
the ocean unlatching its wavelets
wave-bracelets unlinking against the coastline
going so far beyond color, the slab-land
bedded with bogs, with edge-tarns
catching up sun, lodged in the land
thrown back from its headlands.
A battlement built of cut boulders.
A shield of larches, bristling.
We were there. The forms fell in.
Shelf-solid and slightly pitched in the plane
the roseate broken-off rocks, tooled or
near-structural, staved at the road's close curves—
the things that were forms
unparceling themselves from their forms
the things that were thrown beneath form
all were the figured entrapped, mid-measure
cyclic, then strange.
We came down, wound down
to the slim beveled beach
slung with the flinting
gradations—rust, grise-rouge, sloe-maroon
selvages of stones, split through, pared off
in cusps, or worn oval bolls,
notions, or shares.

Acknowledgments

Many thanks to the editors of the journals in which some
of these poems first appeared: the *Canary, Chicago Review,
Colorado Review, Columbia Poetry Review, jubilat,* the *Literary
Review, Underwood: A Broadside Anthology, Verse, Volt,* and
1913: A Journal of Forms.

A selection of the poems was published by Sara Langworthy
in a limited edition titled *Morpho Terrestre.*

I am very grateful to the National Endowment for the Arts for
its support while finishing this work.

Colophon

This book is typeset in Arno Pro, by Robert Slimbach, and Quadraat, by Fred Smeijers, fonts based on humanist types designed in Europe in the fifteenth and sixteenth centuries. The handmade paper that was scanned for the cover was made at the University of Iowa Center for the Book from flax and abaca fibers.